Hope you have an exotic journey with Lavender!

Discover Cooking
with
Lavender

By
Kathy Gehrt

Kathy Gehrt 2010

Photography by
BRIAN SMALE

FLORENTIA PRESS • SEATTLE, WASHINGTON

Cover design by Mary Workman

Page layout by Frances Robinson

Food design by Shelley Thomas

Photography by Brian Smale

ISBN-13 978-0-615-30696-4

ISBN-10 0-615-30696-9

First Edition: January 2010

Printed in China

10 9 8 7 6 5 4 3 2 1

Library of Congress Control Number: 2009940326

CONTENTS

ACKNOWLEDGMENTS

CREATING THIS BOOK HAS BEEN AN ADVENTURE. The journey began when my friend Kris Dews suggested the topic. Kris approaches cooking with an artistic perspective, creating unique flavor combinations. Experimenting with lavender, Kris discovered new techniques for extracting flavor from this exotic herb. I thank Kris for inspiring me to embark on this journey.

Lavender growers from Sequim, in the northwest corner of Washington State, to Kula, a district in the upcountry of the Hawaiian island of Maui, all played a part in supporting this book. I am grateful to: The Lavender Sisters, Katy Jo Steward, Dana Illo and Merrilee Runyan; Cynthia Johnson of Fox Farm; Catherine MacNeal and Tom Dalzell of Lavender Hill Farm; Mary Borland of Olympic Lavender Farm; Susan Harrington of Labyrinth Hill Lavender; Barbara Hanna of Lost Mountain Lavender; Ali'i Chang and Lani Weigert of Ali'i Kula Laven-

Acknowledgments

der (AKL); Ellen Spector Platt of Meadow Lark Flower & Herbs; and Virginia McNaughton of Lavender Downs.

The photos were taken at Crescent Falls Organic Farm, Fox Farm (*owner Cynthia Johnson is pictured on left*) and Lavender Hill Farm on Vashon Island near Seattle, Washington. Credit for these photographs goes to my friends, award-winning photographer Brian Smale, and food stylist Shelley Thomas, who created the settings, suggested props and designed the shots. I appreciate their talent. A special thank you goes to Kate Moffitt and Charlotte Rose Smale for participating in this project.

Mary Workman used her artistic talent to create the cover and suggest the design for the book's interior. Frances Robinson supported this project with her excellent design and editing skills, enthusiastic support and friendship.

My Wednesday writing group—Debra Daniels-Zeller, Sandra Earle, Wendy Hinman, Elsie Hulsizer, Sheila Kelly, Sharon Morris and Jan

Acknowledgments

Schwert—offered support for this project and provided valuable critique. I am grateful for their high standards. Roberta Cruger and Theo Pauline Nestor, writing coaches, have generously shared their time and talent.

Lastly, I want to thank my husband, John. When we married many years ago, he could not have imagined he would be tasting lavender in dishes such as Roasted Halibut *à la Provence* and drinking lavender martinis. John has accompanied me on lavender junkets in California, Washington and Hawaii. I love him and the many adventures we have taken together.

INTRODUCTION

PEOPLE ASK ME HOW I DISCOVERED COOKING WITH LAVENDER. Like many culinary discoveries, this one sprang from a love of food, friendship and gardening, along with a bit of whimsy.

A lavender bush dominated my small p-patch garden at the community farm. Surrounded by bright red poppies, the evergreen lavender plant spread itself out and reached up toward the summer sky. The colors were stunning, scarlet poppies with black centers curled up close to the purple-crowned bush. Exuberant and lively, this lavender plant was big and bold. Bees busily gathered the sweet nectar, white butterflies fluttered around. I was captivated. It was love at first sight and smell, although the first taste was yet to come.

Fresh, flavorful food has always been a part of my life. My parents introduced me to wholesome food. We always had a family garden, where we raised carrots, tomatoes, cucumbers, corn and Swiss chard. Raspberries and strawberries ripened on the vine in our backyard. My dad fished for salmon, trout and steelhead in Puget Sound and the Green River. What we did not grow or catch ourselves, we bought at nearby farms

Introduction

in the Puyallup Valley. My family loved food and took time to enjoy it.

Both my mother and father were adventurous cooks. My dad's lemon meringue pie is a vivid and sweet memory; however, his signature dish was an onion omelet with the unfortunate name of "Onion Gush Gush." My mom's specialties were spaghetti and meatballs, turkey soup and cinnamon rolls. In her late seventies, she entered her cinnamon rolls in competition at the Puyallup Fair; she won a blue ribbon. With eight children to feed, my parents knew the value of using each season's abundance. When apples were ripe, we ate apple pie and apple crisp. When strawberries were in season, jam and shortcake were on the menu.

My passion for fresh food and my discovery of lavender paired up like long-lost lovers in the summer of 2004 when I indulged my fascination with cooking by assisting at cooking classes. A chef I met that summer shared her enthusiasm for cooking with lavender.

I was intrigued and began to research techniques for introducing lavender's fragrance and flavor to everyday cooking. I pored over cookbooks and experimented with techniques and flavor combinations. Over the next two years,

Introduction

I tested recipes using lavender in everything from lavender ginger lemonade to lavender roasted salmon. I found that lavender brings out the fruity taste of berries, grapefruit and pears. I learned how to toast dried lavender buds to achieve a rustic, earthy taste for savory dishes. I discovered how to make flavored sugars, syrups and herbal seasoning blends, making it easy for lavender to come to our dinner table.

I use fresh, natural ingredients, enjoying simplicity and unique flavors. My recipes were selected for their flavors, ease of preparation and use of local, organic foods.

A renewed interest in lavender is evident around the globe; lavender is now celebrated at festivals from Washington state to Michigan and from Australia to Japan. People grow this herb on large and small farms. Some harvest the flowers and sell them at farmers' markets; others isolate lavender oil to use in soap, lotion and perfume; and many harvest and use lavender buds for culinary creations. Beekeepers collect honey made by bees that pollinate the lavender plant's showy flowers.

Whether you love to cook, enjoy new flavors or just like reading about new culinary techniques, I want to welcome you to the world of cooking with lavender!

Kathy Gehrt
Seattle, Washington

From Garden to Table

LAVENDER'S VIVID COLOR AND ENTICING FRAGRANCE tantalize us from gardens around the globe. Hardy and evergreen, this plant flowers in summer. Easy to grow, it has only two essential requirements—full sun and well-drained soil. In return, it offers showy buds, intoxicating aroma and exotic flavor. Bees buzz around its blossoms and gather its sweet nectar and white butterflies flutter from flower to flower. As if being beautiful, fragrant and easy-to-grow weren't enough, lavender also delivers fresh vibrant flavor when used in cooking.

Lavender, like most culinary herbs, belongs to the mint family. This family shares distinctive traits such as square stems, equal and opposite leaves and lipped flowers. Many members of this family, such as rosemary, basil, thyme and sage, are known for their bright flavor and taste.

The Kitchen Garden

A sunny spot in the garden near the kitchen door is the perfect place for an herb garden. If sun is lacking near your kitchen, choose the next best spot you can find—in your garden, on a deck or near your driveway.

Include lavender with other culinary herbs such as rosemary, thyme, mint and tarragon. English lavender is the best for culinary use; among the many varieties, my favorites are Hidcote, Munstead and Royal Velvet. If you have limited space, you may want to plant your herbs in a container with good drainage. Whether in a container or in your garden, an herb garden makes it easy to add a sprig of rosemary or a few lavender buds to your culinary creation.

Using Fresh Lavender

Fresh lavender will enliven your recipes. To remove the lavender blossoms, rub your fingers from the bottom of the stem to the top, pulling off the flowers.

Fresh lavender flowers are less concentrated than dried lavender, so you will need nearly twice as much to get the same amount of flavor. When considering fresh lavender versus dried, use this guideline: Two teaspoons fresh lavender = ¾ teaspoon dried lavender = ¼ teaspoon powdered lavender.

Harvesting and Drying Lavender

When lavender is blossoming, you can cut spikes when the first bud is starting to open. Harvest the lavender in the mid-afternoon when the flowers are dry. Cut the spike down near the first leaf. Create a small bunch of spikes and hold them together with a rubber band. Using paper clips, hang the bunch on a line or rack in a warm, dark and dry spot such as a garage, basement or shed. Allow about a week for the lavender to dry. When fully dried, pack bunches away in a paper bag to keep the dust off. To remove the buds, place the dry lavender sprigs between your hands and rub back and forth over a shallow bowl or a kitchen towel until the buds drop off. Store the buds in an airtight container. Dried lavender keeps for months if stored in a dark and dry place. I save small jars to fill with lavender buds. A jar of homegrown lavender buds together with a favorite recipe makes a thoughtful gift.

Other Places to Find Culinary Lavender

Culinary lavender is also available from lavender growers, spice stores and at grocery stores. In late summer, some lavender farms open their fields for U-Pick. This is a fun and inexpensive way to get lavender if you don't want to grow your own.

Spice stores also offer dried lavender buds. *Penzeys Spices*, *The Spice House*, *Market Spices* and *World Spice Merchants* are only a few of the many shops and websites selling culinary lavender. These stores and lavender growers also sell dried lavender buds online. See page 135 for contact information or search the internet for "culinary lavender buds" for a list of suppliers. Local Harvest (www.localharvest.org) will provide a list of growers near you. Some grocery stores also offer culinary lavender buds. Look for the buds in the bulk food section.

Cooking with Lavender

The pungent flavor of herbs has inspired cooks for centuries. Medieval monks were among the first to embrace herbs, and they turned cooking with them into a culinary art. Apothecary gardens within the monasteries provided herbs for cooking and also for natural medicine. Lavender, once used almost exclusively for healing and cleansing, also became popular in teas, jellies and candies. In France, lavender is a popular culinary herb, but it is less well known in America. However, our consumption of herbs and spices has reached an all-time high, reflecting our enjoyment of varied flavors, appreciation of Asian and Latin American foods, and our interest in experimenting with new herbal fusions.

Use Lavender Judiciously

Lavender offers a zesty flavor, so a little goes a long way. Start with a small amount, then add more until you are satisfied with the taste. Use lavender as an accent. It should enhance the other flavors in the dish, not overpower them. Lavender may be the star in the garden, but in the kitchen, this herb's job is to bring out the best in others.

Basic Cooking Techniques

Flavoring food with lavender is easy. Three techniques and several basic recipes will get you started.

1. **Infusions.** Soak or steep lavender buds in hot water, then remove the buds; the water or liquid will retain a hint of the flavor. This lavender liquid can serve as the basis for herbal tea (by adding mint and chamomile), lavender syrup or lavender lemonade. Milk or cream infused with lavender adds an exotic taste to ice cream or whipped cream. Honey, applesauce or even vodka can be infused with the flavor of lavender.

2. **Baking.** For baking, add lavender to dry ingredients. An easy way

to add the taste of lavender to pastries is to grind the buds in a food processor. Add a pinch of the ground buds to your cookie dough, cake batter or coffee cake mix. Lavender pairs well with chocolate, ginger, lemon or blueberries. I like to substitute lavender for cinnamon in some recipes. In the next chapter, you will find recipes for several lavender sugars and savory seasonings.

3. Dry Roast to Create Herbal Blends. Roasting dried lavender buds transforms the taste of lavender from slightly floral to rustic and earthy, making it perfect for savory dishes such as *Roasted Lavender and Hazelnut-Encrusted Salmon* (page 89). These seasoning blends may be prepared and kept on hand in your pantry for up to a year. Be sure to label and date the container and keep in a cool, dark place.

To roast lavender, you will need 2 cups of dried culinary lavender buds and a 12-inch skillet. Put lavender buds in the skillet and cook over high heat, stirring occasionally for 1 to 2 minutes. Remove the skillet from the heat. Set aside to cool.

Many cooks like to use herb blends to create unique tastes. The French are particularly expert at this technique. *Herbes de Provence*, a blend of dried herbs that originated in Southern France, traditionally includes thyme, rosemary, bay and fennel. This combination provides a starting point for creative cooks to add or substitute other herbs to suit their palates. The addition of lavender, mint or citrus zest can create an entirely new taste sensation.

Bouquet garni is a small bundle of fresh herbs such as thyme, parsley, bay leaf and the like that can be tied in a cheesecloth bag and used for flavoring soups and stews. Once again, the French deserve the credit for this culinary technique. I sometimes add a sprig of lavender to my *bouquet garni* when poaching chicken to create a subtle zesty taste.

Fines herbes—freshly harvested and finely chopped herbs—is another way to enjoy a blend of flavors. This classic combination includes tarragon, chives, parsley and chervil. Because these herbs quickly lose their flavor, they are added just before serving. A pinch of chopped lavender blossoms added to *fines herbes* and blended with the other herbs gives sauces, meat and fish a fresh, bright taste.

Sugars, Seasonings, Blends & More

WHY NOT ENJOY SUMMER'S BOUNTY THROUGHOUT the year? With these easy recipes you can savor the taste of lavender anytime.

When summer has faded, lavender's flavor and aroma can be captured in pantry staples such as lavender sugar, seasoning blends and infused honey. Lavender sugar sprinkled on top of a pink grapefruit can take you back to midsummer, and during the holiday season, lavender-infused treats make inexpensive and unique gifts for teachers, neighbors or friends.

Lavender Sugar MAKES 2 CUPS

Easy to make, lavender sugar can be used in countless ways. It is delicious sprinkled on strawberries or added to a cup of tea.

1 tablespoon lavender buds
2 cups granulated sugar, in all

1. Put lavender buds and ¼ cup of the granulated sugar in a spice grinder or clean coffee grinder; blend for about 1 minute, or until the mixture is a soft powder.
2. Add the lavender buds and sugar mixture to the remaining 1¾ cup sugar.
3. Place sugar mixture in a container with a tight-fitting lid. Allow to sit for three days before using to infuse the sugar with the lavender flavor.
4. As a variation, you can make lavender sugar by layering the lavender buds and sugar in a jar, then straining out the buds when you use the sugar, or place whole sprigs of lavender in a jar with sugar.

Tip: To clean your coffee grinder, add ¼ cup uncooked rice to your grinder. Pulse on and off about 10 times. Discard the rice, then use a damp cloth to wipe out the grinder to remove any remaining traces of coffee.

Lavender Vanilla Sugar   MAKES 2 CUPS

Fresh and mellow flavors complement each other when lavender and vanilla are combined. Use this sugar in cookies, quick breads or sprinkled on your morning toast.

1 vanilla bean
Lavender Sugar (recipe on page 11)

1. Slice vanilla bean lengthwise. Scrape the seeds into a container of lavender sugar, then add the vanilla bean. Seal tightly.
2. Store for at least 1 week before using to allow the sugar to absorb the vanilla and lavender flavors.

Lavender Ginger Lemon Sugar   MAKES 2 CUPS

Enjoy flavored sugars on muffins, as well as sprinkled on fresh pears or berries.

½ cup sugar
½ teaspoon lemon zest
1 tablespoon crystallized ginger, chopped
1½ cups Lavender Sugar (recipe on page 11)

1. In a spice grinder or clean coffee grinder, combine ½ cup sugar, lemon zest and crystallized ginger. Grind into a powder.
2. Stir mixture into 1½ cups lavender sugar.
3. Store in an airtight container.

13

Lavender Salt

MAKES ½ CUP

Rub this seasoned salt on chicken, fish or lamb for a savory and slightly sweet taste.

½ cup sea salt
2 teaspoons dried lavender buds, finely ground

1. Combine sea salt and ground lavender buds.
2. Use immediately or store in an airtight container.

Lavender Pepper

MAKES ¼ CUP

Rub lavender pepper on a steak before grilling, or sprinkle on fish, chicken, salad or eggs. Red peppercorns add a sweet fruity taste that balances the pungent black peppercorns; green peppercorns taste light and fresh. Look for a variety of peppercorns and granulated citrus peel in spice shops.

1 tablespoon dried lavender buds
1 tablespoon fine sea salt
1 tablespoon black peppercorns
¼ teaspoon green peppercorns
¼ teaspoon red peppercorns
¼ teaspoon white peppercorns
1 tablespoon fennel seeds
1 teaspoon granulated lemon peel
1 teaspoon granulated orange peel
4 whole allspice berries

1. Place all ingredients in a spice grinder or food processor and blend until as coarse as ground pepper.
2. Store in an airtight container.

Tuscan Seasoning

MAKES 2 CUPS

Mix this seasoning with butter or olive oil and spread on a fresh baguette for delicious lavender garlic bread.

½ cup roasted lavender (instructions on page 6)
¼ cup dried onion flakes
¼ cup dried minced garlic
1 tablespoon salt

1. Place all ingredients in a food processor or blender. Process for 10 seconds, or until all ingredients are well blended.
2. Store seasoning in an airtight container.

Mediterranean Seasoning

MAKES 2 CUPS

Add a zesty taste to roasted vegetables with this savory blend.

½ cup roasted lavender buds (instructions page 6)
¼ cup dried basil
¼ cup dried cilantro

1. Place all ingredients in a food processor or blender. Process until well blended, about 10 seconds
2. Store seasoning in an airtight container.

Latin Seasoning

This seasoning adds a smoky taste to fish, pork, chicken and eggs. The color comes from achiote rojo *paste. Found in most Mexican grocery stores, the paste's main ingredient is annatto seeds, which are prized in Indian and Hispanic cuisine for their slightly bitter, earthy flavor and russet color.*

2 tablespoons cumin seeds

1 tablespoon coriander seeds

2 tablespoons dried lavender buds

2 tablespoons dried thyme leaves

2 tablespoons *achiote rojo* paste

1 tablespoon freshly ground black pepper

½ teaspoon fine sea salt

1. In a dry skillet, toast the cumin, coriander and lavender over medium heat until fragrant, about 2 minutes. Cool.
2. Using a spice grinder or clean coffee grinder, pulse the mixture until finely ground.
3. Transfer the mixture to a food processor and add the thyme, *achiote rojo* paste, pepper and salt. Pulse to blend completely.
4. Store in an airtight container.

Fines Herbes

MAKES ½ CUP

Fresh lavender adds a slightly floral note to this combination of light and sweet herbs. Use them to enhance omelets and sauces. Choose fresh herbs for this recipe.

3 tablespoons Italian parsley
2 teaspoons fresh lavender buds
1 tablespoon chives
1 tablespoon tarragon
1 teaspoon chervil

1. Finely chop and combine all the herbs.
2. Sprinkle on food just before serving.

Herbes de Provence

MAKES 1 CUP

This mixture of dry herbs may be used to season meat, poultry, fish and vegetables.

5 tablespoons dried thyme
3 tablespoons dried savory
2 tablespoons dried marjoram
5 tablespoons dried rosemary
1½ tablespoons dried lavender buds

1. Use a fork to mix all of the ingredients together in a small bowl.
2. Store in an airtight container.

Bouquet Garni   MAKES 1 HERB BUNDLE

An herb bouquet infuses soups, stews and sauces with flavor. Create a bundle of fresh herbs and tie them together with kitchen twine, or wrap them in cheesecloth so you can remove the bundle before serving. This works especially well for poaching halibut.

2 fresh parsley sprigs
1 dried bay leaf
1 fresh sprig of thyme
1 fresh sprig of lavender
1 fresh fennel frond

1. Gather herbs into a small bundle. Tie them together with kitchen twine, or wrap them in cheesecloth held together with the twine.
2. Add the bundle to soups, stews or poaching liquids; remove bundle before serving.

Gremolata

A gremolata is a mixture of finely chopped ingredients used as a topping to add extra flavor to savory dishes. Typically served on osso buco (braised veal shanks), this herbal seasoning also gives grilled fish a bright fresh taste.

1 tablespoon fresh parsley, chopped

2 cloves garlic, finely chopped

1 teaspoon lemon zest

¼ teaspoon dried lavender buds, finely ground, or 1 teaspoon fresh lavender buds, chopped

1. Blend all ingredients together.
2. Sprinkle on fish, chicken or meat just before serving.

Lavender-Infused Honey

MAKES 1 CUP

Lois Franz (pictured on left) became intrigued with bees when, as a school girl, she read a story about a sister and brother who meet a fairy. The fairy changes herself and them into bees and invites the bee-children into a hive where she explains how honey is made. "I was hooked," Lois says.

The years flew by as she and her husband raised seven daughters. When Lois finally found some time to call her own, she studied beekeeping. She now manages her own hives and shares her knowledge and enthusiasm for bees at schools, farmers' markets and festivals. Following is Lois' recipe for lavender honey.

1 cup locally-produced mild honey (such as clover, blackberry or alfalfa)
¼ cup dried lavender buds

1. Combine honey and dried lavender buds in an 8-ounce jar.
2. Cover the jar and let the honey sit on your kitchen counter for about a week; this allows the lavender to release its flavor.
3. Every day for a week, turn the jar upside down to keep the buds submerged in the lavender. They will have a tendency to float to the top, so turning the jar over once a day will keep the buds covered with honey.
4. After 1 week, remove and discard lavender buds by filtering honey through a fine strainer (or several layers of cheesecloth) into a clean jar. Cover, and store at room temperature.

Hazelnut and Dried Fruit Topping   MAKES ABOUT 1 CUP

You'll love this topping on your morning toast or muffin.

½ cup hazelnuts, roasted and cooled, coarsely chopped
¼ cup dried cranberries, coarsely chopped
¼ cup dried apricots, cut into ½-inch pieces
½ cup Lavender Honey (recipe on page 25)

1. Stir nuts and fruits together, then spoon the mixture into an 8-ounce glass jar.
2. Pour honey over the mixture and cover.
3. Store in the refrigerator for up to one month. Bring to room temperature before serving.

Honey Lavender Butter Spread MAKES 4 OUNCES

Sweet flavored butter turns a simple piece of toast or a warm muffin into an extra special treat.

½ cup butter, at room temperature

¼ cup honey

¼ teaspoon lavender, finely ground

1. Mix all ingredients together until smooth.
2. Place in a ramekin or small bowl and store covered in the refrigerator.

Savory Lavender Butter Spread MAKES 4 OUNCES

Lavender butter is a wonderful partner for fish and grilled meats—a delicious and easy way to bring lavender to the table.

1 tablespoon chives
1 tablespoon chervil
½ cup unsalted butter, at room temperature
1 teaspoon dried lavender buds, finely ground
1 tablespoon lemon juice
Salt and pepper

1. Chop chives and chervil finely, then use a spatula to combine them in a small bowl with butter, lavender and lemon juice. Add salt and pepper to taste.
2. Roll mixture in plastic wrap or parchment paper to form a cylinder about 1½ inches in diameter. Refrigerate for 1 hour, or place in the freezer for 30 minutes.
3. To use, remove wrap from roll and slice into ¼-inch-thick rounds.

Lavender Vinegar

MAKES 3 CUPS

Vinegar provides another way to preserve the taste of fresh lavender. Use it to give salad dressings, sauces and marinades a fresh flavor.

1 cup fresh lavender sprigs
3 cups white vinegar
6 (4-inch-long) fresh lavender sprigs

1. Place 1 cup lavender in a 1-quart glass jar. Pour vinegar over lavender, cover, and set jar aside in a cool place for 3 to 4 weeks.
2. Strain vinegar from jar and discard used lavender.
3. Put 6 new lavender sprigs in a 1-quart bottle. Pour the strained vinegar into the bottle and seal with a cork. The vinegar will keep its flavor for up to six months.

Apple Lavender Jelly   MAKES 4 (6-OUNCE) JARS

Sweet and delicate, this simple jelly lets us enjoy the taste of apples and lavender's fragrance all year round. Use organic, locally-grown apples for best results. You can use any variety of apples; Fuji, Rome and Delicious all work well.

> **6 pounds apples**
> **1½ cups fresh lavender buds, or 2 tablespoons dried buds**
> **½ cup water**
> **3 cups sugar (amount may vary depending on juice yield from apples)**
> **½ cup crème de cassis or Grand Marnier liqueur**
> **Cheesecloth**

1. Quarter apples (don't peel or core) and place them in a large saucepan along with the lavender and water. Bring to a boil and simmer until apples are tender, about an hour.
2. Line a colander with three layers of cheesecloth, and place colander over a large bowl.
3. Pour apple mixture into the cheesecloth and allow the juice to drip overnight. In the morning you will have approximately 3 cups of juice, depending on the juice content of your apples.
4. Sterilize 4 (6-ounce) jars.
5. Pour juice into a large saucepan. Add sugar, using 1 cup of sugar for each cup of juice.

6. Bring juice and sugar to a rapid boil. Continue boiling until the temperature reaches 220°F, or a drop of the juice forms a hard film on a cold spoon.
7. Stir liqueur into hot juice.
8. Pour hot mixture into sterilized jars and seal with paraffin.

Lavender Syrup MAKES 1 CUP

Sugar, water and lavender create a tantalizing syrup to drizzle over fresh fruit or to add to iced tea or lemonade.

1 cup water
1 cup sugar
2 tablespoons fresh, or 1 tablespoon dried, lavender
1 strip lemon zest

1. Combine water and sugar in a small saucepan. Boil mixture until the sugar dissolves.
2. Remove the syrup from the heat and add lavender and lemon zest. Allow to steep for 30 minutes to infuse the sugar water with flavor.
3. Strain the liquid into a jar with a tight-fitting lid. Store in the refrigerator until ready to use.

Blueberry Lavender Syrup Makes 1½ cups

Lavender and blueberries were meant for each other. These flavors are wonderful individually, and when they are combined, the taste offers something special. Delicious over ice cream, pound cake or waffles.

¾ cup water

½ cup sugar

4 teaspoons dried lavender buds or ¼ cup fresh lavender flowers

2 teaspoons fresh lemon juice

1 pint fresh blueberries, washed and dried

1. Mix water and sugar together in a small saucepan. Stir over medium heat until the sugar is dissolved.
2. Bring mixture to a boil, then remove from heat.
3. Stir in lavender; allow to steep for 30 minutes.
4. Pour the syrup through a fine sieve to remove the lavender buds. Discard the buds.
5. Stir lemon juice and blueberries into the syrup. Store in the refrigerator for up to 1 week.

Candied Lavender Wands

Makes 6 TO 12 WANDS

These sweet wands taste like candy. They make fun stirring devices or edible garnishes for iced tea or lemonade

6 to 12 fresh lavender stems, with leaves removed
½ cup Lavender Syrup (recipe on page 32)
½ cup Lavender Sugar (recipe on page 11)

1. Dip lavender stems in the lavender syrup.
2. Roll the dipped stems in the lavender sugar.
3. Place the sugared lavender wands on parchment paper and let dry for at least 1 hour.

DELECTABLE DRINKS

WHETHER IT'S IN A TALL, COOL, SUMMER DRINK OR a steaming mug of cider, lavender adds an exotic flavor. The simplicity of steeping lavender buds in wine, juice, milk or water makes it easy to create fresh, vibrant flavor in lemonade, cocoa, smoothies and cocktails.

The next time you entertain friends or host a family picnic, add a special touch by serving a lavender-infused drink. Raise a glass to this fragrant herb!

Lavender Lemonade MAKES 6 TO 8 SERVINGS

Nothing says summer like lemonade. It is simple, delicious and refreshing. Lavender adds a slightly floral taste that makes it special.

> 1½ cups boiling water
> ¼ cup dried lavender buds or ½ cup fresh lavender blossoms
> 1 (12-ounce) can frozen lemonade
> 2 cups cold water

1. Add lavender buds or blossoms to boiling water and let mixture steep (sit in a covered pan) for 20 minutes.
2. Strain mixture to remove lavender buds or blossoms, then set aside the lavender-infused water and let it cool to room temperature.
3. Add the frozen lemonade and 2 cups of cold water to the cooled lavender-infused water.
4. Mix well and chill.

Honey Ginger Lavender Lemonade   Makes 6 servings

*Full of flavor, lemonade is a welcome refreshment on a summer day.
Add a shot of vodka for an adult cocktail.*

3 cups water, divided
½ cup honey
½ cup sugar
¼ cup fresh ginger, peeled and minced
1 tablespoon dried or fresh lavender buds
1¼ cups fresh lemon juice
Ice cubes

1. Combine 1 cup water, honey, sugar, ginger and lavender in a heavy medium saucepan. Boil for 5 minutes, stirring occasionally to dissolve sugar. Let cool for 30 minutes.
2. Strain cooled syrup into a 2-quart pitcher.
3. Mix in lemon juice and the remaining 2 cups of water. Fill pitcher with ice cubes. Let stand for 5 minutes.
4. Fill 6 tall glasses with ice, then fill them with lemonade. Garnish with lemon slices and fresh lavender flowers.

Lavender Lemon Soda

Fizzy, sweet, cold and fresh, soda tastes great on a hot summer afternoon. Hidcote lavender is a great choice for this drink because of its floral essence. Blue Velvet, Provence or Munstead varieties also work well.

1 cup water
1 cup sugar
2 tablespoons fresh lavender flowers
1 cup freshly-squeezed lemon juice
25.3 fluid ounces sparkling mineral water
Ice cubes

1. Combine water, sugar, and lavender in a small saucepan and bring to a simmer over gentle heat.
2. Remove pan from stove and let mixture steep for 5 to 10 minutes. Strain out flowers and chill the syrup until you are ready to use it.
3. Combine lavender syrup with lemon juice and pour ½ cup of this liquid into an ice-filled glass. Fill the glass with sparkling mineral water and stir. Serve immediately.

Her Majesty's Tea

MAKES 2 SERVINGS

Queen Elizabeth I loved lavender tea. She drank as many as ten cups a day "to ward off headaches and promote a sense of well being." For a variation, you may want to combine the lavender with chamomile, mint, or a small amount of rosemary.

2 tablespoons fresh lavender buds
2 cups boiling water
Sugar, honey, or lemon (optional)

1. Place fresh lavender buds into a tea ball.
2. Pour boiling water into a ceramic tea pot, then add tea ball. Set pot aside for 5 minutes, then remove tea ball.
3. Pour tea into cups and add sugar, honey or lemon according to individual taste.

Spiced Cranberry Cider Mix   Makes 12 to 14 servings

Hot cider is a great winter drink to enjoy after skiing, snowshoeing or a neighborhood walk. Pack the dry mix into a decorative jar and attach a note with serving directions for a tasty gift.

½ cup dried cranberries
12 cinnamon sticks
½ teaspoon crushed whole cloves
2 tablespoons whole allspice
1 tablespoon dried lavender buds

1. Mix cranberries, cinnamon sticks, cloves, allspice and lavender buds together in a small bowl.
2. Pack mixture into an airtight container to store.
3. When ready to serve, prepare according to the directions for Spiced Cranberry Cider (following page).

Spiced Cranberry Cider   MAKES 12 TO 14 SERVINGS

2 quarts apple cider
1 quart water
1 jar Spiced Cranberry Cider Mix (see previous recipe)
2 oranges, thinly sliced

1. Combine the cider, water and Spiced Cranberry Cider Mix in a large saucepan. Heat, but do not boil.
2. Add most of the orange slices, reserving enough for a garnish for each cup.
3. Pour warm mixture into cups or mugs. Garnish with remaining orange slices and serve.

Josephine's Hot Chocolate

Lavender was the secret ingredient in the nightcap Josephine created for Napoleon. Not only delicious, this drink always seemed to put Napoleon in a "romantic" mood. Serve on Valentine's Day and add a small amount of liqueur for a special touch. Josephine added an ounce of coffee to her potion.

3 cups whole milk or half-and-half

2 teaspoons dried lavender buds

1 ounce bittersweet chocolate, chopped

1 tablespoon Dutch-process cocoa powder

2 tablespoons sugar

$^1/_8$ teaspoon kosher salt

½ teaspoon pure vanilla extract

1. Pour milk into a medium saucepan and stir in lavender buds. Set over medium heat and bring just to a boil.
2. Remove mixture from heat and steep for 3 to 5 minutes, or longer for a stronger lavender flavor.
3. Strain the milk to remove the lavender buds, and then pour the milk back into the saucepan. With the saucepan over medium heat, whisk in the chopped chocolate until melted and smooth.
4. Whisk in the cocoa powder, sugar, and salt; remove from heat and whisk in the vanilla extract.
5. Divide among coffee mugs. Top with whipped cream or a home-made marshmallow (recipe follows).

Homemade Espresso-Flavored Marshmallows

Light, fluffy and delicious, marshmallows are easy-to-make. These treats bring a rich sweet taste to hot chocolate.

2 (¼-ounce) envelopes unflavored gelatin

½ cup cold espresso

¾ cup hot water

2 cups granulated sugar

1 cup light corn syrup, divided

¼ teaspoon salt

1 teaspoons vanilla

½ cup powdered sugar

½ cup cornstarch

1. Lightly coat a 9-inch square baking pan with butter; set aside.
2. In a small bowl, combine gelatin and cold espresso. Stir with a spoon until the mixture gets very thick. Let stand for 5 minutes.
3. In a 2-quart saucepan, combine hot water, ½ cup of corn syrup and granulated sugar. Place over high heat and stir with a wooden spoon until the mixture begins to boil. Wash down sides of saucepan with a wet pastry brush to eliminate sugar crystals.
4. Clip a candy thermometer onto the side of the saucepan and cook the mixture to 238°F, or the soft ball stage.

5. Remove from heat and stir in remaining corn syrup. Pour mixture into a medium-sized bowl. Using an electric mixer on high speed, beat hot syrup and add gelatin mixture 1 tablespoon at a time. Continue beating until all the gelatin is incorporated and the mixture is thick and has cooled to lukewarm. This will take about 10 minutes.

6. Stir in vanilla and salt, then pour into prepared pan. Cool 3 hours, or until marshmallow is firm enough to cut.

7. Using a knife dipped in hot water, cut marshmallows into pieces about 1¾ inches square.

8. Combine powdered sugar and cornstarch and sprinkle mixture over the marshmallows to keep them from sticking.

Blueberry Solstice Smoothie   MAKES 1 SERVING

Blueberries and lavender are a winning combination in this healthy drink. Try it for a mid-morning energy boost.

8 ounces vanilla yogurt
½ cup blueberries, fresh or frozen
2 teaspoons Lavender Sugar (recipe on page 11)
3 ice cubes

1. Place yogurt, berries, lavender sugar and ice cubes in blender.
2. Blend on high for 45 seconds.
3. Pour into a glass and enjoy.

Lavender Mulled Wine MAKES 6 SERVINGS

Mulled wine is warm and comforting when the weather turns cool. It is great for sipping while sitting by the fireplace.

> 1 bottle dry red wine (merlot or cabernet sauvignon both work well)
> ½ cup Lavender Sugar (recipe on page 11)
> 1 cinnamon stick
> 6 allspice berries
> 2 whole cloves
> 2 strips lemon zest
> 2 strips orange zest
> 1 sliced lemon or orange
> Additional cinnamon sticks for garnish

1. Combine the wine, lavender sugar, cinnamon, allspice, cloves and lemon and orange zests in a large saucepan.
2. Bring to simmer over medium heat, then cook for 5 minutes.
3. Strain into mugs and garnish with lemon or orange slices and cinnamon sticks.

Honey Lavender Summer Gin MAKES 2 SERVINGS

Enjoy the sweet taste of the season with an easy and delicious cocktail that is perfect for a summer celebration.

¼ cup hot water
1 teaspoon dried lavender buds or 1 tablespoon fresh lavender
    blossoms
¼ cup honey
6 tablespoons gin
2 tablespoons freshly-squeezed lemon juice
Ice cubes

1. Steep lavender blossoms in hot water. Set aside for 5 minutes.
2. Whisk honey into water and lavender mixture.
3. Pour mixture through a strainer into a small bowl to remove the lavender blossoms.
4. Add gin and lemon juice. Pour into a cocktail shaker filled with ice cubes.
5. Shake well and strain into two chilled martini glasses.

Raspberry Lavender Cooler   Makes 4 servings

An easy, fresh and delicious drink that will delight your guests!

1 (10-ounce) bag frozen raspberries, thawed
¼ cup fresh orange juice
¼ cup Lavender Syrup (recipe on page 32)
1 bottle white wine, chilled
4 lavender sprigs, for garnish
Fresh raspberries, for garnish

1. Combine thawed raspberries, orange juice, lavender syrup and wine in a blender.
2. Blend for 1 minute, or until mixed.
3. Pour into glasses and garnish with lavender sprigs and fresh raspberries.

Midsummer Berry Bliss   Makes 6 servings

In this version of a margarita, raspberries and blueberries join tequila, coconut milk, and a hint of lavender to make a fruity and exotic adult smoothie.

½ cup tequila
¼ cup blue Curaçao or other orange-flavor liqueur
½ cup canned coconut milk (stir before measuring)
4 tablespoons fresh lime juice
1 cup frozen unsweetened raspberries
1 cup frozen blueberries
2 cups ice cubes
1 tablespoon granulated sugar
1 teaspoon fresh or dried lavender blossoms
Lime wedge
Rinsed lavender sprigs (optional)

1. Combine tequila, Curaçao, coconut milk, and lime juice in a blender. Add cover and blend on high speed for 30 seconds.
2. With blender running, gradually add raspberries, blueberries and ice cubes. Blend until slushy and smooth, 2 to 3 minutes.
3. Mix sugar and lavender blossoms in a small bowl. Rub with your fingers or mash with a spoon to release the lavender flavor. Rub glass rims with lime wedge to moisten, and then dip rims into lavender-sugar mixture, coating them evenly.
4. Pour margaritas into glasses. Garnish with lavender sprigs.

Lavender Lemon Drop

Try this variation on a classic cocktail. The lavender sugar on the rim adds a hint of summer sunshine.

1 tablespoon Lavender Sugar (recipe on page 11)
1 tablespoon freshly-squeezed lemon juice
4 ounces (½ cup) citrus vodka
2 tablespoons triple sec orange-flavored liqueur
Ice cubes

1. Rub glass rims with lemon wedge to moisten, and then dip rims into lavender sugar mixture, coating them evenly.
2. Pour vodka and triple sec into 16-ounce cocktail shaker two-thirds full of ice cubes. Shake for 15 seconds.
3. Strain and pour mixture into two stemmed cocktail glasses.

Lavender Gin or Vodka   Makes 1 (750-milliliter) bottle

Make your next cocktail a gin (or vodka) and tonic à la Provence with lavender-infused spirits, then imagine yourself visiting the French countryside, celebrating the sweet life.

1½ teaspoons dried lavender buds
1 (750-milliliter) bottle gin or vodka

1. Add lavender to gin or vodka, letting its flavor infuse for 1 day.
2. Strain out lavender. Use the liquid to make your favorite cocktails.

Lemon Lavender Martini

A sophisticated, quintessential cocktail gets a fresh and fragrant new taste.

   4 ounces (½ cup) vodka
   2 ounces (¼ cup) Lavender Syrup (recipe on page 32)
   1 ounce (2 tablespoons) freshly-squeezed lemon juice
   Ice cubes

1. Pour vodka, lavender syrup, and lemon juice into a cocktail shaker.
2. Add ice cubes and shake for 15 seconds.
3. Strain into two chilled martini glasses.
4. Garnish each glass with a fresh sprig of lavender.

Lavender Cosmopolitan MAKES 2 SERVINGS

Parfait Amour—a sweet liqueur made from Spanish oranges, vanilla, rose and almond—gives this drink a purple hue. Lavender sugar on the rim of the glass makes it festive and flavorful.

> 1 tablespoon freshly-squeezed lime juice
> 1 tablespoon Lavender Sugar (recipe on page 11)
> 2 ounces (¼ cup) citrus vodka
> 2 ounces (¼ cup) *Parfait Amour*
> 2 ounces (¼ cup) cranberry juice
> 2 slices lime
> Ice cubes

1. Rub the rim of your martini glass with lime juice then dip it into a saucer of lavender sugar.
2. Pour vodka, *Parfait Amour* and cranberry juice into a cocktail shaker, then add 1 cup of ice cubes and shake for 15 seconds. Strain into two chilled martini glasses.
3. Garnish each glass with a sprig of fresh lavender and a slice of lime.

Summer Sangria Punch Makes 7 to 8 (6-ounce) servings

Perfect for a summer party, this festive drink tastes fruity and refreshing. Cool and colorful, sangria's deep and complex flavor adds a sophisticated touch. To reduce the alcohol content, add more fruit juice.

1 (750-milliliter) bottle Chianti

4 ounces (½ cup) brandy

4 ounces (½ cup) triple sec

4 ounces (½ cup) Lavender Syrup (recipe on page 32)

4 ounces (½ cup) fresh orange juice

4 ounces (½ cup) cranberry juice

2 oranges, cut into 1/8-inch slices

2 lemons, cut into 1/8-inch slices

1. Combine all ingredients in large pitcher or bowl then cover and refrigerate for at least 4 hours.
2. Pour the punch into a punchbowl or serving pitcher. Add orange and lemon slices for a garnish.
3. Serve in wine glasses.

Savory Creations

VALUED FOR THEIR FRAGRANT FLAVORS, HERBS boost and brighten vegetables, meat, poultry and fish. In this chapter, you will find recipes for appetizers, salads, soups, side dishes and entrées.

When our food delivers full-bodied flavor, our appetite celebrates and our hunger is sated. When you try these recipes, you will discover how even a small amount of lavender can bring out the best in other ingredients.

Tapenade with Capers and Lavender   MAKES 2 CUPS

This tapenade is as colorful as the Italian flag and an easy crowd pleaser. The artichokes stand in for the traditional olives and the Mediterranean flavors create a taste sensation. Serve on crostini or artisan crackers. Marian Robertson's tapenade (from Cooking Gluten-Free *by Karen Robertson) was the inspiration for this version.*

1 jar (7 ounces) roasted red peppers, drained

1 can (6 ounces) whole artichokes, drained and quartered

½ cup fresh Italian parsley, large stems removed

1 teaspoon Mediterranean Seasoning (recipe on page 18)

½ cup Parmesan cheese, grated

¼ cup extra-virgin olive oil

3 cloves garlic, finely chopped or passed through a garlic press

1 tablespoon lemon juice

¼ cup capers, drained

1. Place all ingredients in a food processor and mix until well blended.
2. Serve on crackers or bread.

Bruschetta with Tomatoes and Roasted Lavender

The word bruschetta comes from the Italian bruscare, *meaning "to roast over coals." Here toasted herbed lavender brings out the sweetness of the tomatoes.*

3 tablespoons extra-virgin olive oil, in all
3 cups vine-ripe tomatoes (2 to 3 medium tomatoes), chopped
¼ cup fresh basil, chopped
1 tablespoon Tuscan Seasoning (recipe on page 17)
2 tablespoons red onion, minced
1½ teaspoons garlic, minced
¾ teaspoon kosher salt
1 loaf rustic artisan bread or a baguette
Black pepper, freshly ground

1. Preheat the barbecue grill or oven broiler to medium-high heat.
2. In a medium bowl, toss together 2 tablespoons olive oil, tomatoes, basil, onion, garlic and salt; set aside.
3. For a baguette-style loaf, use a serrated knife to cut it into 12 (½-inch) slices. For a wide loaf, cut it into 6 (½-inch) slices, then slice each piece in half to make 12 pieces in all.
4. Brush both sides of the bread with the remaining tablespoon of oil, then grill on each side until lightly marked or toasted.
5. Place toasted bread on a platter and immediately top with the reserved tomato mixture and sprinkle with black pepper.

Fresh Pickled Vegetables

MAKES ABOUT 2 QUARTS

Crispy, colorful, and packed with flavor, these vegetables are irresistible. Keep on hand in the refrigerator for a quick and nutritious snack, or add them to just about any lunch or dinner menu for a refreshing change from cooked vegetables.

½ cauliflower

2 carrots

2 celery stalks

1 green pepper

1 red pepper

6 mushrooms

½ red onion

¼ cup green and/or black olives

Brine

½ cup oil (half extra-virgin olive oil and half salad oil)

½ cup rice vinegar

¼ cup red wine vinegar

1 teaspoon salt

1 teaspoon lavender buds

1 teaspoon oregano

2 tablespoons sugar

⅛ teaspoon freshly ground black pepper

1. Cut cauliflower, carrots, celery, peppers, mushrooms and red onion into bite-size pieces.
2. Add ½ cup water to large sauté pan, cover and bring to boil. Add cauliflower, carrots and onion and cook for 1 minute. Using a slotted spoon, remove vegetables and place them on a paper towel to cool. Repeat process for green peppers, mushrooms and red peppers.
3. Meanwhile, place all ingredients for the brine in a saucepan. Over medium heat, bring the mixture to a boil and cook for 5 minutes.
4. Place vegetables and olives in large bowl or a 2-quart jar with a tight fitting lid. Pour vinegar mixture over vegetables. Chill before serving.
5. Store in refrigerator for up to one week.

Crispy Pickled Carrots   MAKES 1 PINT (8 TO 10 SERVINGS)

Bright, crispy orange carrots make a healthy appetizer or a great addition to any meal. Keep them in the refrigerator for a quick snack.

1 pound carrots, peeled and cut lengthwise into ½-inch-thick sticks
4 fresh lavender sprigs with blossoms, each about 4 inches long
   (or ¼ teaspoon dry lavender buds)
¾ cup rice or white wine vinegar
½ cup sugar

1. Trim carrot sticks so they fit vertically in a 1-pint glass jar, about ¾-inch below the rim.
2. In a 10 to 12-inch frying pan, bring about 1 inch of water to boiling over high heat. Add carrots and cook uncovered until they are barely tender when pierced, about 5 to 7 minutes; drain.
3. Lay jar on its side and pack carrots in loosely so that they will be standing upright in the jar; tuck fresh lavender sprigs between carrots. (If you are using dried lavender buds, sprinkle the buds over the carrots.)
4. In a 1 to 1½-quart pan, combine vinegar and sugar and bring to a boil. Stir until sugar dissolves, then pour hot liquid over vegetables to cover. Reserve extra liquid.
5. Cover jar with lid and shake jar to release any trapped bubbles.
6. Chill until next day, then check jars and add reserved marinade, if needed, to cover vegetables.
7. Chill in the refrigerator up to 2 weeks, turning jar occasionally.

Grilled Pear Crostini

MAKES 12 CROSTINI

Crostini, meaning "little toasts" in Italian, are frequently served as appetizers. Combining pears, lavender and goat cheese creates a pleasing flavor fusion, especially when served with a cold white wine such as Pinot Grigio.

2 red pears, still firm
1 tablespoon extra-virgin olive oil
1½ tablespoons lavender buds, chopped or finely ground in a spice grinder
4 ounces goat cheese
1 baguette, cut into 12 slices, ¼-inch thick

1. Peel and core pears, then slice them into ¼-inch thick rings.
2. Rub rings with olive oil and 1 tablespoon ground lavender buds.
3. Grill rings over medium heat. Turn once after pear is softened and has grill marks, about 2 minutes. Cook another 2 minutes. Remove rings from grill and cut each ring in half.
4. Grill baguette slices, turning once until slightly toasted, about 1 minute.
5. Spread bread with goat cheese and top with pear slices.
6. Place crostini on a platter and sprinkle with remaining ½ tablespoon chopped lavender.

Ginger Carrot Soup

Bright is the word that best describes this soup. The orange color is festive and appealing, and the flavor has sweet, citrus, and tangy layers.

1 tablespoon butter
½ cup minced onion
¼ cup fresh ginger, peeled and minced
1 teaspoon Lavender *herbes de Provence* (recipe on page 21)
3 cups chicken stock or canned low-salt chicken or vegetable broth
4 cups (about 1½ pounds) carrots, peeled and sliced
¼ cup orange juice
$1/_8$ teaspoon curry powder
¼ teaspoon salt
$1/_8$ teaspoon pepper
Chives

1. Heat butter in a heavy large saucepan over medium-high heat. Add onion, ginger and *herbes de Provence*. Sauté until onion is translucent, about 5 minutes, then add chicken stock and carrots. Cover and simmer until carrots are tender, about 45 minutes.
2. Working in batches, puree mixture in a blender or processor, then return pureed soup to saucepan. Stir in orange juice. Cook over low heat for 5 minutes.
3. Mix in curry, salt and pepper and bring to simmer; thin with more stock if needed. Ladle into bowls; garnish with snipped chives.

Provence Potato Soup MAKES 6 SERVINGS

In this rustic soup, bacon adds a subtle smoky flavor and the potatoes offer comfort as well as nutritional value. Dried herbs, commonly found in Southern France, are combined into a seasoning called herbes de Provence, *a blend that is easy to make or you can buy it at your grocery store.*

3 thick slices bacon, cut into ¼-inch pieces
1 large yellow onion, finely chopped
1 clove garlic, minced
2 carrots, peeled and finely chopped
2 celery stalks, finely chopped
2 teaspoons *herbes de Provence* (recipe on page 21)
½ teaspoon salt
1 teaspoon freshly ground black pepper
4 cups low-sodium vegetable or chicken stock
3 pounds (about 4 cups) russet potatoes, peeled and cut into
    ½-inch cubes
2 tablespoons snipped fresh chives (optional)

1. Cook bacon pieces in a large saucepan over medium heat until the fat is released, about 5 minutes.
2. Sauté onion, garlic, carrots and celery in the bacon fat. Add *herbes de Provence*, salt and pepper. Cook until the vegetables are soft, about 7 minutes.

3. Add the stock, and bring mixture to a boil.
4. Add the potatoes, and return to a boil. Allow mixture to cook for 3 minutes, stirring often.
5. Reduce heat and let mixture simmer, uncovered, until potatoes are soft and can easily be pierced with a fork, about 15 to 20 minutes.
6. Serve in small bowls, garnished with chives.

Roasted Butternut Bisque with Curried Yogurt Topping

MAKES 10 CUPS

Thick and creamy bisque will warm you up on a cold winter day. Freeze leftovers in small containers for a quick and satisfying snack.

2 butternut squash (about 4 pounds total)
1 small garlic bulb (whole bulb—not individual cloves), unpeeled
1 large onion, chopped
3 carrots, sliced
1 tablespoon extra-virgin olive oil
2 teaspoons Lavender *herbes de Provence* (recipe on page 21)
4 cups vegetable broth
Chives for garnish

For topping
½ cup nonfat yogurt
½ teaspoon curry powder

1. Preheat oven to 350°F.
2. Cut butternut squash in half (do not remove seeds yet) and place both halves cut side down on a rimmed baking sheet.
3. Halve garlic bulb crosswise, then place the halves back together and wrap them tightly in foil. Place on baking sheet along with squash, and place baking sheet in hot oven. After 30 minutes, care-

fully turn squashes halved-side up and continue cooking until soft, about 20 more minutes.

4. Meanwhile, sauté onion and carrots in oil in a saucepan over low heat until softened, about 10 minutes.

5. When squash is done, scoop out the seed section and throw it away, then scoop out squash and add it to the saucepan. Unwrap garlic and squeeze the soft garlic out of the cloves into the saucepan.

6. Add vegetable broth and lavender *herbes de Provence* to the squash and garlic; stir to combine.

7. Bring squash mixture to a boil, then reduce heat to a simmer. Use an immersion blender to puree the contents of the saucepan, or puree in batches in a food processor or blender.

8. To make the topping, blend curry into yogurt.

9. Ladle hot bisque into bowls and top with curried yogurt. Sprinkle with snipped chives.

Grilled Shrimp, Avocado and Grapefruit Salad

MAKES 4 ENTRÉE SALADS

This classic combination brings together plump pink shrimp, vibrant grapefruit, and the cool green of the lettuce and avocado. The sweet shrimp and tart grapefruit are perfect partners for the avocado and lettuce.

2 pink or red grapefruits

¼ cup fresh grapefruit juice

⅓ cup extra-virgin olive oil

1 tablespoon lime juice

Salt and pepper, to taste

16 medium shrimp (about 1 pound), shelled and deveined

1 tablespoon Latin Seasoning (recipe on page 19)

1 tablespoon vegetable oil

1 head butter lettuce, separated into leaves, then washed and dried

3 tablespoons fresh tarragon leaves, chopped

3 tablespoons fresh chives, chopped

3 tablespoons fresh chervil leaves, chopped

2 firm, ripe avocados, peeled and cut lengthwise into ¼-inch slices

1. Using a sharp knife, cut the peel from the grapefruit, then, holding the peeled grapefruit over a bowl to catch the juice, cut out the segments. Leave grapefruit pieces in the bowl and strain juice into a measuring cup to remove the seeds.

2. Squeeze the remaining grapefruit juice from the pith and membranes and strain it into the measuring cup as well. You will need ¼ cup of juice for the dressing.

3. Stir olive oil, lime juice and salt into the grapefruit juice to make a vinaigrette; set aside.

4. Use a paper towel to pat shrimp dry, then coat them with Latin seasoning.

5. Heat oil in skillet over moderately high heat until hot, but not smoking. Sauté shrimp until pink and just cooked through, about 3 minutes. Set aside.

6. In a large bowl, combine butter lettuce and chopped herbs. Pour half of the vinaigrette over the lettuce mixture and season with salt and pepper.

7. Using tongs, gently lift the lettuce and herbs out of the bowl, dividing evenly onto four plates.

8. Add shrimp and avocado slices to the bowl of grapefruit segments. Drizzle remaining vinaigrette over the mixture. Toss gently, then divide evenly on top of the lettuce on each plate.

Pear Salad with Arugula, Romaine and Blue Cheese Dressing

Red Anjou pears make a colorful and tasty salad and the lavender pepper in the dressing goes nicely with the blue cheese. Lavender pepper is a great staple for your pantry. You can buy it from the Cedarbrook Lavender & Herb Farm (see The Lavender Pantry, page 135) or make your own at home.

1 bunch arugula, torn

1 head romaine lettuce, torn

3 medium red Anjou pears, cored and thinly sliced

1 cup buttermilk

1 cup blue cheese crumbles

½ teaspoon Lavender Pepper (recipe on page 15)

1 ounce (about 3 tablespoons) walnuts, chopped and toasted

1. Place arugula, romaine and pears in a large bowl.
2. Combine buttermilk, blue cheese and lavender pepper, then pour dressing over salad and toss.
3. Sprinkle walnuts on top.

Roasted Romaine with Lavender Vinaigrette

A warm medley of chunky vegetables makes a salad that can be served as an entrée or a first course. The roasting process boosts the flavors.

2 portabella mushrooms
1 head romaine lettuce, washed and dried and cut in half
    through the core
1 red bell pepper, cut into ½-inch pieces
2 medium tomatoes, cut into ½-inch chunks
1 whole sweet onion, sliced into ½-inch rings
6 tablespoons extra-virgin olive oil
1 tablespoon Tuscan Seasoning (recipe on page 17)
1 tablespoon balsamic vinegar
1 tablespoon freshly-squeezed lemon juice

1. Remove stems from the mushrooms. Clean the mushrooms with a brush, then place them on a hot grill or hot dry frying pan over high heat. Roast for 3 minutes on each side. Remove from grill or pan and set aside.
2. Place romaine lettuce, cut side down, on a hot grill or hot dry frying pan. Roast for 1½ minutes on each side or until lettuce has grill marks. Remove from pan and set aside.
3. Grill bell pepper, turning every minute until grill marks appear on each side. Set aside.

4. Grill onion rings, for 30 seconds on each side. Set aside. All vegetables should have grill marks on the outside, but remain slightly raw on the inside.
5. Combine olive oil, Tuscan seasoning, vinegar and lemon juice. Set aside.
6. Cut roasted vegetables into large chunks and place in a salad bowl. Add tomatoes and dressing and toss lightly.

Roasted Vegetables
with a Hint of Lavender

Colorful and healthy, veggies have never tasted better! The marinade brings in the fresh, bright taste of lavender in a subtle yet distinctive way. Pure lavender honey is available from many lavender growers who keep bees in their field, or you may infuse your own Lavender Honey.

2 red bell peppers

1 green bell pepper

2 onions

2 small zucchini

8 ounces mushrooms

6 new potatoes, scrubbed

3 garlic cloves, crushed

1 yellow squash

Marinade

1 tablespoon thyme

1 tablespoon rosemary

½ cup Lavender Honey (recipe on page 25)

1½ teaspoons marjoram

1 garlic clove, minced

1 shallot, minced

¼ cup aged balsamic vinegar

Olive oil

Savory Creations

1. Preheat oven to 425°F.
2. Cut vegetables into 1-inch pieces.
3. Mix marinade ingredients together in a large bowl, then add cut vegetables and toss to coat.
4. Coat a rimmed baking sheet with olive oil.
5. Place vegetables on pan; sprinkle with salt and pepper.
6. Bake in oven for 30 minutes, or until vegetables are fork-tender.

Smashed Potatoes

What can be more satisfying than creamy potatoes? Infused with a trace of garlic and lavender and topped with butter and sour cream, these are an excellent accompaniment to steak, salmon or chicken.

1¾ pounds small Yukon Gold potatoes, scrubbed, peels left on
6 large garlic cloves, peeled
1 teaspoon lavender buds, dried or fresh
1 teaspoon salt
1 tablespoon extra-virgin olive oil
2 tablespoons (¼ stick) butter
½ cup sour cream
3 tablespoons fresh chives, chopped
Salt and pepper, to taste

1. Place potatoes, garlic, lavender and salt in a medium pot. Cover with water and cook until potatoes are tender, about 20 to 30 minutes. (Cooking time will vary depending on size of potatoes.) Drain; let stand 5 minutes, then discard garlic and lavender buds.
2. Generously butter glass pie pan, then arrange potatoes closely together in the pan. Using a wooden spoon, smash potatoes coarsely until they split open. Drizzle with olive oil and dot with butter. Sprinkle with salt and pepper.
3. Preheat broiler. Broil potatoes until crisp and golden, about 8 to 10 minutes. Watch closely to avoid burning!
4. Top with dollops of sour cream and sprinkle with chives.

Mediterranean Rice Pilaf with Basil and Pine Nuts

Pilaf is a perfect partner for roasted fish. Basil and the Mediterranean seasoning add a zingy flavor, while the pine nuts add a little crunch.

1 (14½-ounce) can chicken broth
1½ tablespoons extra-virgin olive oil
½ large onion, chopped
1 cup long-grain rice
⅓ cup fresh basil, chopped
1 teaspoon Tuscan Seasoning (recipe on page 17)
¼ cup pine nuts, toasted
Salt and pepper, to taste

1. Bring broth to a simmer in a small saucepan; reduce heat to low and keep warm.
2. Meanwhile, heat oil in another small heavy saucepan over medium heat. Add onion and sauté until translucent, about 6 minutes.
3. Add rice to oil and stir for 1 minute.
4. Add warmed broth to rice and oil mixture and bring to a boil, then reduce heat to low. Cover and cook until broth is absorbed and rice is tender, about 20 minutes.
5. Stir basil, Tuscan seasoning, and pine nuts into rice.
6. Season with salt and pepper. Serve hot.

Couscous with Spring Vegetables
Makes 4 servings

Pearl couscous, also called Israeli couscous, makes a nice change of pace from rice, pasta or orzo. This dish delivers an assortment of textures and flavors.

3 tablespoons extra-virgin olive oil, divided

1 cup pearl couscous, uncooked

2 cups vegetable broth

1 avocado, peeled, pitted and diced

1 cucumber, peeled, seeded and chopped

1 cup cherry tomatoes, halved

1 cup grilled asparagus, cut diagonally into ½-inch pieces

¼ cup dried cranberries

½ cup pine nuts

16 Kalamata olives

Juice of 1 lemon

½ cup red onion, finely chopped

1 shallot, finely chopped

1 teaspoon dried lavender buds, finely ground

¼ cup Italian parsley, coarsely chopped

1. Add 1 tablespoon of the olive oil to a medium saucepan. Heat to medium-high, then add couscous, stirring until the couscous is lightly toasted, about 2 minutes.

2. Add vegetable broth; cover and simmer for 15 minutes.
3. Strain couscous and set aside to cool.
4. Combine avocado, cucumber, tomatoes, asparagus, dried cranberries, pine nuts and olives in a large bowl, then fold in the cooled couscous.
5. Combine remaining 2 tablespoons extra-virgin olive oil with lemon juice, onion, shallot, lavender and parsley.
6. Pour the olive oil mixture over couscous and toss lightly.
7. Serve at room temperature.

Roasted Lavender and Hazelnut-Encrusted Salmon

Salmon is abundant in the Pacific Northwest. Add local lavender and hazelnuts to give it a rustic texture and earthy flavor.

¼ pound hazelnuts
1 teaspoon roasted lavender (instructions on page 6)
1 teaspoon fresh basil
1 garlic clove, minced
1 pound salmon fillet, 1-inch thick
1 tablespoon honey
1 tablespoon Dijon mustard
Lemon wedges for garnish

1. Preheat oven to 375°F. Place hazelnuts in a single layer on a rimmed jelly roll pan and bake in oven for 5 to 7 minutes, stirring occasionally. Remove from oven to cool.
2. In a food processor, chop hazelnuts coarsely, then combine them in a small bowl with the lavender, basil and garlic.
3. Coat salmon with honey, then brush on Dijon mustard.
4. Put salmon fillet on a baking sheet or cedar plank and coat with hazelnut mixture. Bake for 25 minutes.
5. Remove salmon from the oven and tent with aluminum foil; let rest for 15 to 20 minutes, then serve with lemon wedges.

Roasted Halibut *à la Provence* MAKES 4 SERVINGS

Sweet, mild halibut accented by colorful red and yellow peppers makes a quick and healthy meal. The lavender seasoning adds a delicate flavor to the firm white fish.

1½ tablespoons extra-virgin olive oil

2 red bell peppers, cored, seeded and cut lengthwise into ½-inch-wide strips

1 yellow bell pepper, cored, seeded and cut lengthwise into ½-inch-wide strips

1 medium onion, slivered (cut onion in half, then across the grain into ¼-inch-wide strips)

1 tablespoon balsamic vinegar

1 tablespoon Mediterranean Seasoning (recipe on page 18)

½ teaspoon kosher salt

¼ teaspoon freshly ground black pepper

3 tablespoons flat-leaf parsley, chopped

1 pound fresh halibut fillet

2 lemons, cut into wedges for a garnish

1. Preheat oven to 400°F.
2. Heat 1 tablespoon of oil in skillet over medium heat. Add peppers and onions and cook for about 10 minutes, stirring often.
3. Add vinegar and Mediterranean seasoning, then cook 15 minutes longer, stirring often.

4. Season with kosher salt, pepper and 2 tablespoons parsley.
5. Spoon vegetables over the bottom of a 9 x 9-inch baking dish.
6. Brush fish with the remaining oil, then sprinkle both sides with salt and pepper.
7. Lay seasoned fish in baking dish on top of vegetables.
8. Bake for 20 minutes.
9. Garnish fish with remaining parsley and lemon wedges. Serve immediately.

Hearty Tuscan Lamb Stew with Lavender

This dish will satisfy meat and potato lovers. The stew simmers for nearly two hours, tenderizing the meat and blending flavors. Serve with crusty bread for soaking up the broth.

2 pounds boneless lamb stew meat, cut into 2-inch cubes

¼ cup flour

½ teaspoon salt

½ teaspoon ground black pepper

4 tablespoons vegetable oil, in all

4 medium carrots, sliced ½-inch-thick

1 medium onion, chopped

4 stalks celery, sliced 1-inch-thick

1 clove garlic

1 tablespoon Tuscan Seasoning (recipe on page 17)

1 cup Syrah or other dry red wine

1½ cups reduced-sodium beef broth

1½ cups water

1 bay leaf

2 cups potatoes, cubed

3 tablespoons flat-leaf parsley, chopped

1. Dredge lamb in flour seasoned with salt and pepper.
2. Pour 1 tablespoon oil into a large heavy skillet over medium-high heat. Add 1/3 of the lamb and cook until browned, about 5 minutes. Transfer meat to a large, heavy Dutch oven. Repeat with remaining meat in 2 more batches, adding 1 tablespoon oil to the skillet for each batch. Transfer browned meat to Dutch oven.
3. Reduce heat to medium and add remaining tablespoon of oil. Add carrots, onion and celery. Stir frequently until vegetables are soft, about 5 minutes.
4. Add garlic and Tuscan seasoning. Cook until fragrant, about 2 minutes. Scrape up browned bits.
5. In Dutch oven, add onion mixture, wine, broth, water and bay leaf to meat and bring to a boil. Cover and simmer, stirring occasionally, until lamb is very tender, about 1½ to 1¾ hours.
6. Add cubed potatoes and cook for an additional 30 minutes.
7. If the broth needs thickening, combine ¼ cup flour with ½ cup cold water. Whisk the flour mixture into the stew and let simmer for 10 minutes.
8. Season to taste with salt and pepper and top with chopped parsley.

Roasted Leg of Lamb

MAKES 8 SERVINGS

Easy, elegant and scrumptious, this dish is perfect for a dinner party or patio supper. The lamb soaks up the lavender-infused marinade, and the result is a tender and palate-pleasing main course.

1 (4-pound) boneless leg of lamb, butterflied
3 tablespoons extra-virgin olive oil
2 tablespoons soy sauce
½ teaspoon lavender buds
1 tablespoon lemon juice
2 cloves garlic, finely chopped
Salt and black pepper

1. Press on the lamb to flatten it, then place it in a large baking dish, boned side up. Make 1-inch slashes in 2 or 3 places at the thickest part of the meat to ensure even cooking.
2. Rub 1 tablespoon of olive oil on the un-boned side of the lamb, then mix the reserved olive oil together with the remaining ingredients and rub it onto the top of the meat. Marinate at room temperature for 1 hour, then remove roast and reserve marinade.
3. Preheat oven to 375°F. Roast lamb for 20 minutes, or until temperature reaches 120°F.
4. Brush lamb with reserved marinade and place it under the broiler for 7 minutes, or until the lamb is browned.
5. Let sit for 8 minutes, then cut into diagonal slices and serve.

Roasted Pork Tenderloin with Garlic and Herb Crust

Pork tenderloin, with its mild flavor and lean meat, is one of my favorites. A savory crust of herbs, garlic, breadcrumbs and olive oil helps keep the tenderloin moist and adds a Mediterranean flavor.

2 tablespoons plain dry breadcrumbs

2 tablespoons Italian parsley, chopped

2 teaspoons lavender buds, finely ground using a spice grinder

2 teaspoons extra-virgin olive oil

1 garlic clove, minced

¼ teaspoon salt

1 pound pork tenderloin, trimmed of all fat

1. Preheat oven to 450°F. Spray a roasting pan with nonstick spray.
2. In a small bowl, combine breadcrumbs, parsley, lavender, olive oil, garlic and salt.
3. Rub the pork tenderloin with the breadcrumb mixture. Place pork in the pan and let sit for 30 minutes to come to room temperature.
4. Roast the pork for 20 to 25 minutes, or until the crust is brown and the pork reaches 160°F. Transfer the roast to a carving board; tent loosely with foil, and let it rest for 10 minutes.
5. Cut into ¼-inch slices and serve with Mediterranean Rice Pilaf (recipe on page 85).

Beef Tenderloin with Red Wine Butter

Beef tenderloin makes an elegant and impressive entrée for a special occasion. The secret to spectacular results is the seasoning, the searing and the sauce. Your guests will be asking for your recipe.

2½ pounds beef tenderloin

1 tablespoon roasted lavender, finely chopped (instructions page 6)

1 tablespoon fresh rosemary, finely chopped

2 tablespoons fresh parsley, chopped

¼ cup extra-virgin olive oil

2 tablespoons bread crumbs

2 cloves garlic, minced

1 teaspoon salt

1 teaspoon pepper

1. Preheat oven to 425°F.
2. Blend all of the ingredients (except the beef) together in a small bowl, creating a thick, paste-like rub.
3. Using a paper towel, pat the beef tenderloin dry. Remove any fat from the beef and coat the tenderloin with the rub, pressing it firmly into the meat. Set aside for 30 minutes, allowing the meat to warm to room temperature.
4. Place an empty roasting pan in the oven for 10 minutes, then remove it from the oven and add 2 tablespoons of olive oil to the

bottom of the pan. Place the tenderloin in the roasting pan and return it to the oven.

5. Sear the tenderloin in the oven for ten minutes on each side, then reduce the oven temperature to 375°F. Cook until the internal temperature is 150°F for rare or 160°F for medium; the topping will be brown.

6. Remove the meat from the oven and place on a carving board. Cover loosely with a foil tent and let it rest for 30 minutes. The temperature will actually rise about another 10 degrees as the cooler center absorbs heat from the outer layers.

7. Slice and drizzle with red wine butter.

Red Wine Butter

2 cups beef broth
1 teaspoon dried lavender buds
2 cups (16 ounces) dry red wine
1 tablespoon tomato paste
2 sticks (8 ounces) butter, at room temperature

1. In a heavy saucepan, combine beef broth, lavender buds, red wine and tomato paste. Bring to a boil and cook for 1 hour and mixture has been reduced to ¾ cup. Cool to room temperature.

2. Whisk butter into the reduced broth, then drizzle mixture over sliced beef.

3. Serve the remaining butter on the side for potatoes.

Sweet Secrets

When my lavender plants are in full bloom in the summer, I am inspired to create desserts flavored with their evocative scent.

I love the simplicity of using lavender in my pastries, the delicate taste it adds to berries and the emphasis lavender adds to chocolate, lemon and cream. I hope you will treat yourself to some of my favorite sweet secrets.

Blueberries Baked in Cream with Polenta Topping

MAKES 6 TO 8 SERVINGS

The inspiration for this dessert came from my mother-in-law, Dorothy. Her blueberry pie scores a perfect ten. To cut calories and time, I eliminated the pie crust. This is a family favorite and always gets raves.

4 cups (2 pints) fresh or frozen blueberries

2/3 cup Lavender Sugar (recipe on page 11)

4 tablespoons flour

½ teaspoon cinnamon

¼ teaspoon salt

½ cup milk

½ cup heavy cream

Polenta Topping

¼ cup flour

$1/_8$ cup Lavender Sugar

$1/_8$ cup coarse polenta

Pinch of cinnamon

Pinch of salt

1 ounce unsalted butter, cold

1. Preheat the oven to 400°F.
2. Rinse berries. After they have drained and are somewhat dry, pour them into a 9-inch buttered ceramic tart pan.

3. Mix together sugar, flour, cinnamon, and salt in a small bowl.
4. Stir the milk and whipping cream into the sugar mixture and whisk until smooth, then pour the mixture over the berries.

For Polenta Topping
1. Blend flour, sugar, polenta, cinnamon and salt together in a food processor.
2. Add butter and pulse until clumps begin to form.
3. Sprinkle polenta mixture on top of the blueberries and cream in the tart pan.
4. Bake for 45 minutes, or until the berry mixture is set.

Lavender Poached Pears

Poached pears can be served at breakfast with yogurt, or as a simple, virtually fat-free dessert when sprinkled with a tiny amount of grated dark chocolate and garnished with a sprig of fresh lavender.

4 small, firm Bosc or Bartlett pears
½ lemon, freshly-squeezed for juice
2 tablespoons lavender buds
5 cups water
⅔ cup sugar
1 tablespoon fresh lemon zest

1. Wash pears, then peel the skin off completely, leaving the stem attached to the pear. (See note below.)
2. Generously rub the pears with lemon juice to prevent them from discoloring.
3. Put the lavender buds in a small piece of cheesecloth and tie up with a piece of kitchen twine.
4. Combine water, sugar, and lavender buds in a large saucepan with a tight-fitting lid; stir until the sugar is dissolved.
5. Bring mixture to a boil, then reduce heat to medium-low and add the peeled pears.
6. Cut parchment paper in a circle the diameter of the saucepan. Place the parchment paper directly on the liquid and pears. Cover the saucepan with the lid.

7. Simmer gently until the pears are tender when pierced with a fork, about 10 to 16 minutes. (The size and ripeness of the pears will determine the cooking time.)
8. Remove the saucepan from the heat and let the pears cool completely in the liquid.
9. Using a slotted spoon, remove the pears to a bowl and set aside.
10. Remove the lavender cheesecloth bundle, then bring the remaining liquid to a boil over high heat. Cook until it is thickened like syrup, about 3 to 5 minutes.
11. Pour the syrup over the pears and refrigerate.

Note: I like to core the pears before cooking. To remove the core (while leaving the stem intact), use a melon baller, apple corer or a small grapefruit knife. From the bottom end of the pear, scoop out the core. Be careful to keep at least ½-inch away from the pear's stem end.

Apple Cherry Turnovers

Apple and dried cherries, flavored with a hint of lavender and wrapped in puff pastry, make a special treat anytime of day. For an elegant dessert, top each turnover with a scoop of ice cream.

1 sheet (8½ ounces) frozen puff pastry, thawed

1 Granny Smith apple

2 tablespoons brown sugar, firmly packed

2 tablespoons Lavender Sugar (recipe on page 11)

¼ teaspoon cinnamon

½ cup dried tart cherries

1. Preheat oven to 425°F.
2. Cut the puff pastry sheet into 4 equal squares and place them on a rimmed baking sheet lined with parchment paper.
3. Peel, quarter, and thinly slice apple into a bowl; sprinkle with sugars and cinnamon, tossing to coat, then add cherries.
4. Place an equal amount of the apple-cherry mixture in the center of each square of dough. Pull one corner of dough over the mixture to meet the opposite corner and form a triangle. Press and seal the two corners together, leaving sides open.
5. Bake until golden brown, about 15 minutes.

Nectarine Gratin with Lavender Honey

MAKES 4 SERVINGS

Lavender honey sweetens and flavors this dessert. Juicy nectarines, sprinkled with sugar, add color, flavor and texture.

Custard

1 cup whole milk

2 large egg yolks, at room temperature

2 tablespoons Lavender Honey (recipe on page 25)

4 teaspoons cornstarch

1 teaspoon pure vanilla extract

Fruit and topping

4 medium-sized fresh nectarines, pitted and cut into $1/8$-inch slices

2 tablespoons sugar

¼ cup hazelnuts, coarsely chopped

1. Heat milk in a small heavy saucepan over medium heat until steaming; remove from heat.
2. Whisk egg yolks, honey and cornstarch in a medium bowl until smooth.
3. Gradually add the hot milk to the yolk mixture, whisking until blended. Return the mixture to the saucepan and cook over medium heat, whisking constantly, until slightly thickened and starting to bubble gently, about 1½ to 2 minutes.

4. Transfer the hot mixture to a clean bowl; whisk in vanilla. Cover loosely and refrigerate until chilled, about 1 hour.
5. To prepare fruit and topping, preheat broiler. Coat an 11 x 7-inch oval gratin dish or 4 individual gratin dishes with cooking spray. Spoon custard evenly into the dish or dishes.
6. Arrange nectarines on their sides, slightly overlapping, in a single layer over custard. Sprinkle sugar and hazelnuts evenly over the nectarines.
7. Broil until nectarines are lightly caramelized, about 5 to 7 minutes. Serve immediately.

Note: Blueberries, plums, raspberries or blackberries can be substituted for nectarines.

Grilled Fruit with Lavender Honey Glaze

Grilling fruit intensifies its flavor, softens the texture and caramelizes the natural sugars. Lavender honey adds an exotic touch. Consider serving this as a luscious ending to a summer meal.

½ cup unsalted butter

½ cup Lavender Honey (recipe on page 25)

1 large ripe pineapple, peeled, quartered, cored, and cut into ½-inch-thick wedges

3 slightly under-ripe bananas, peeled and sliced in half lengthwise

3 ripe but firm peaches, peeled, halved, pitted, and cut into quarters

1 pint vanilla ice cream (optional)

1. Combine the butter and lavender honey in a small saucepan. Heat, whisking occasionally, until the butter is melted and the mixture just comes to a simmer.
2. Preheat a gas grill to medium.
3. Brush each piece of the fruit with the glaze.
4. Place the fruit on the grill and cook, turning once, until the fruit is heated through, slightly tender and caramelized. This will take about 4 minutes total for the bananas, and 6 minutes for the pineapple and peaches. You can also grill the fruit in a grill pan or skillet on your cooktop.
5. Serve immediately, with a scoop of vanilla ice cream if desired.

Deep-Dish French Toast with Blueberries and Lavender

Looking for a special breakfast or brunch recipe? This oven-baked French toast combines bread, eggs, milk and sugar with cream cheese, blueberries and nuts. The secret ingredient—lavender—makes all the other ingredients taste even better, a great dish for an Easter buffet.

1 teaspoon butter for coating the baking dish

1 large (1½ to 1¾-pound) brioche loaf cut into 1-inch cubes, about 10 cups

1 (8-ounce) package cream cheese, cut into 18 cubes

¾ cup pecans, chopped

½ cup blueberries

8 large eggs

2 cups milk

½ cup dark brown sugar, firmly packed

2 teaspoons pure vanilla extract

½ teaspoon lavender buds, ground into powder

Pinch of nutmeg

Pinch of ground cloves

4 tablespoons butter, melted

Serve with

Powdered sugar

Pure maple syrup, warmed

1. Butter a 9 x 13-inch baking dish. Place half the bread cubes in a single layer, covering the bottom of the dish. Scatter the cream cheese cubes, nuts, and blueberries on top. Cover with the remaining bread cubes.

2. In a large bowl, whisk together the eggs, milk, brown sugar, vanilla, lavender, nutmeg, and cloves. Pour this mixture evenly over the bread cubes. Press down on the bread cubes to make sure they absorb the egg mixture. Cover with plastic wrap and refrigerate for four hours or overnight. To ensure bread absorbs the egg mixture, put a heavy item (e.g., two pounds of butter) on top of the plastic wrap to weigh down the bread.

3. Heat the oven to 350°F. Remove the dish from the refrigerator and let it sit for 20 minutes at room temperature.

4. Bake the French toast covered for 20 minutes, then uncover it and bake 15 to 20 minutes longer, or until the cubes are nicely toasted.

5. Place the dish on a cooling rack, then drizzle the melted butter over the French toast. Let sit for 5 minutes. Cut into squares.

6. Sprinkle powdered sugar over the top and serve with warm maple syrup.

Lavender Sugared Puffed Pancake with Berry Compote

MAKES 2 LARGE SERVINGS

Puffed pancakes, sometimes known as Dutch Babies or German pancakes, are baked pancakes traditionally made with cinnamon and vanilla. In this version, lavender adds a fresh flavor and Berry Compote makes a luscious topping.

2 large eggs

¼ cup Lavender Sugar (recipe on page 11)

⅓ cup whole milk

½ cup all-purpose flour

1 tablespoon butter

1 teaspoon ground lavender

½ tablespoon powdered sugar

1 tablespoon freshly-squeezed lemon juice

Berry Compote

2 cups mixed berries, fresh or frozen

1 cup sugar

1. Preheat oven to 425°F.

2. Mix the eggs and lavender sugar together in a medium bowl. Add the milk, continuing to mix. Sift the flour into the mixture and mix with a whisk until the batter is smooth. Set the batter aside and let

it rest for 5 minutes.

3. Melt the butter over medium heat in a 10-inch ovenproof skillet, then pour the batter into the skillet and let it cook without stirring for 3 minutes.

4. Place the skillet in the center of the oven to bake until the edges become brown and the center puffs up, about 14 minutes.

5. Remove the skillet from the oven. (Be sure to use good oven mitts, the skillet will be hot!)

6. Sift the lavender and the sugar over the pancake, then drizzle with lemon juice.

For Berry Compote

1. Stir berries and sugar together in a saucepan and heat slowly on low heat until sugar dissolves, about 5 minutes.

2. Spoon onto pancake or serve in a bowl to pass around for individual servings.

Strawberries with Lavender Yogurt Cream

MAKES 6 SERVINGS

Lavender brings out the sweetness of the strawberries in this delicious recipe adapted from The Provence Cookbook *by Patricia Wells.*

1 pound fresh strawberries, stemmed and cut into sixths
1 tablespoon balsamic vinegar
1 tablespoon Lavender Sugar (recipe on page 11)

Lavender Yogurt Cream

1 cup Greek-style yogurt
2 tablespoons crème fraiche or heavy cream
1 tablespoon Lavender Honey (recipe on page 25)
6 sprigs of lavender, for garnish

1. Chill 6 desert goblets by placing them in the refrigerator.
2. Combine the strawberries, vinegar and lavender sugar; stir gently. Cover tightly with plastic wrap and refrigerate for 30 minutes. Just before serving, combine the yogurt and crème fraiche in a bowl and whisk gently, adding 1 tablespoon of lavender honey, or to taste. The mixture will remain quite firm.
3. Spoon the strawberries into the goblets and top with the Lavender Yogurt Cream. Garnish each goblet with a sprig of lavender.

Crunchy Granola Makes about 11 cups

Lavender brings out the sweetness of the blueberries and cranberries in this crunchy granola recipe from the Vashon Island Lavender Harvest Celebration. Thanks go to Denise Kitchel for the recipe.

½ cup vegetable oil
½ cup honey
1 cup golden brown sugar, firmly packed
1 tablespoon pure vanilla extract
1 tablespoon finely ground lavender
½ teaspoon salt
8 cups old-fashioned style rolled oats
1½ cups mixed nuts (almonds, cashews and macadamia nuts)
½ cup sweetened flaked coconut
1 cup dried blueberries
1 cup dried cranberries

1. Preheat oven to 325°F.
2. Combine the oil, honey, brown sugar, vanilla, lavender and salt in a large saucepan set over medium heat. Stir until the sugar dissolves, about 3 minutes.
3. In a large bowl, combine the oats, nuts and coconut. Pour the warm oil and honey mixture into the oat mixture and stir until combined.
4. Spread the mixture evenly on two 12 x 17-inch rimmed baking

sheets.

5. Bake for 20 to 30 minutes, stirring several times, until the granola is deep golden brown.
6. Cool completely before adding the dried fruit.
7. Store in an airtight container for up to 3 weeks.

Variations: "Fruits and nuts can be changed to include whatever you have on hand," says Denise, "that's the wonderful thing about granola. Candied ginger or citrus peel, for instance, are really nice with lavender."

Blueberry Cheesecake Bars

These cheesecake bars are packed with flavor. The nutty crust complements the cream cheese topping, which is infused with lavender and studded with juicy blueberries. You will need about a cup, in all, of lavender sugar for this recipe.

For crust

½ cup butter

¾ cup graham crackers, finely crushed

½ cup all-purpose flour

½ cup flaked coconut

½ cup pecans, finely ground in a food processor

¼ cup Lavender Sugar (recipe on page 11)

For topping

12 ounces cream cheese, softened

⅔ cup Lavender Sugar

4 eggs

1 tablespoon milk

1 teaspoon pure vanilla extract

2 cups fresh blueberries

1. Preheat oven to 350° F.
2. Lightly grease 13 x 9 x 2-inch baking pan, then line pan with parchment paper, leaving an inch hanging over each side; set aside.

3. For crust, heat butter in small saucepan over medium heat until the color is like light brown sugar. Remove from heat; set aside.
4. In a medium bowl, stir together graham crackers, flour, coconut, pecans, and ¼ cup lavender sugar; stir in the melted butter until combined.
5. Evenly press the graham cracker mixture into the bottom of the prepared pan. Bake 8 to 10 minutes or until lightly browned.
6. While the graham cracker mixture is baking, beat cream cheese and ⅔ cup lavender sugar until combined using an electric mixer on medium speed. Add eggs, milk, and vanilla. Beat again until combined.
7. Pour the cream cheese mixture over the hot crust and sprinkle the top with blueberries.
8. Bake 18 to 20 minutes or until the center appears set.
9. Cool in pan on rack, then cover and refrigerate.
10. Refrigerate for several hours, then lift edges of parchment paper to remove from the pan. Cut into bars. Store covered in refrigerator.

Lemon Lavender Pound Cake   MAKES ABOUT 12 SERVINGS

The pound cake originated in 17th century England. The original recipe called for one pound each of butter, sugar, eggs and flour. As baking powder and baking soda came into use in the late 1800s, the recipe was modified. Lemon gives this cake a citrus taste, while lavender adds a hint of fresh flowers.

4 cups all-purpose flour

½ teaspoon baking powder

½ teaspoon baking soda

½ teaspoon salt

1 tablespoon dried lavender buds, finely ground

8 ounces unsalted butter, at room temperature

2¼ cups granulated sugar

3 tablespoons freshly-grated lemon zest

5 eggs

¼ cup freshly-squeezed lemon juice

1 cup plain sour cream

For the glaze

1 cup powdered sugar

2 teaspoons freshly grated lemon zest

2 tablespoons freshly-squeezed lemon juice

1 teaspoon dried lavender buds, finely ground using a spice grinder

Sweet Secrets

1. Preheat the oven to 325°F. Butter and flour a 12-cup Bundt pan.
2. Sift flour, baking powder, baking soda, and salt into a large bowl. Stir in the dried lavender buds, then set mixture aside.
3. Combine butter, sugar, and lemon zest in the bowl of a stand mixer. Using the paddle attachment, mix on medium speed until the mixture becomes smooth and pale, about 5 to 8 minutes.
4. Add eggs, one at a time, fully mixing each into the batter before adding another. After the last egg is added, slowly add the lemon juice and mix for 1 minute. Scrape down the sides of the bowl and mix 30 more seconds until all ingredients are fully incorporated.
5. Remove bowl from the mixer. Add flour mixture in 3 parts, alternating with the sour cream. Use a rubber spatula and gently mix just until all ingredients are incorporated.
6. Pour batter into prepared Bundt pan, filling pan two-thirds full.
7. Bake on center rack of oven for 70 minutes, or until the top is golden brown. Insert a tooth pick into the center of the cake; it will come out clean when the cake is done.
8. Let cake cool in the pan on a wire rack for at least 20 minutes.
9. Loosen the sides of the cake with a sharp knife. Place serving plate, upside down, on the top of the cooled Bundt pan and invert the pan to remove the cake. Let cake cool completely.

Glazing the cake

1. Sift powdered sugar and ground lavender buds into a medium bowl, and then add lemon zest and lemon juice. Mix with a spoon until smooth. Drizzle glaze over the cooled pound cake.

Lavender and Orange Glazed Pecans MAKES 2 CUPS

The recipe for this appetizer was created by Susan McRae of California Lavender. I like to serve this during the winter holidays; the taste of lavender and oranges in the dark of winter is a sensual reminder of summer.

2 cups pecan halves (about ½ pound)
1 cup Lavender Sugar (recipe on page 11)
¼ cup orange juice
1 tablespoon grated orange zest
½ teaspoon dried ginger

1. Lightly toast pecans in large heavy pan over low heat.
2. Line cookie sheet with waxed paper.
3. Bring sugar, orange juice, orange zest and ginger to a boil in a large heavy saucepan over medium heat, stirring constantly. Boil 30 seconds. Stir in pecans.
4. Spread pecans in one layer on waxed paper and cool completely.
5. Separate pecans if necessary and store in an airtight container.

Note: Prepare this recipe 1 day to 1 week ahead. The lavender sugar should be made at least 3 days before using to allow time for the lavender to infuse its flavor into the sugar. Sift the sugar to remove the lavender buds before adding it to the recipe.

Lavender Spritz Cookies   MAKES ABOUT 48 COOKIES

This delicate butter cookie originated in Scandinavia and is traditionally served during the Christmas season. Use a cookie press to make festive shapes such as snowflakes, wreathes or kisses. Lavender sugar gives these classic cookies a new twist. Sanding sugar is available in many colors—including lavender—at most grocery stores.

> 2¼ cups all-purpose flour
> ¾ cup Lavender Sugar (recipe on page 11)
> ½ teaspoon salt
> ¼ teaspoon baking powder
> 1 cup unsalted butter, at room temperature
> 1 large egg
> 1 egg white (for egg wash)
> 1 teaspoon pure vanilla extract
> Sanding sugar*

1. Preheat oven to 375°F.
2. In a medium size bowl, mix together the flour, sugar, salt and baking powder. Using two knives or a pastry blender, cut the butter into the flour mixture until it looks like coarse crumbs.
3. Break the egg into a measuring cup and add enough water to make 1/4 cup; beat the egg and water together.
4. Add the egg/water mixture and the vanilla to the crumb mixture; mix with a fork until the cookie dough begins to stick together.

5. Put the dough into a cookie press and press onto cookie sheets. (Hint: Chilling the cookie sheets helps the cookie press to release better shaped cookies.)
6. With a fork, mix together 1 egg white and 1 tablespoon water.
7. Brush the egg white mixture onto each cookie, then sprinkle with sanding sugar.
8. Bake for 10 to 12 minutes or until very light brown. Cool on a baking rack.

*Note: Sanding sugar is an edible, large-crystal sugar that does not dissolve when heated. Sometimes called pearl-sugar or decorating sugar, it adds "sparkle" to baked goods because the sugar crystal grains are large and reflect light.

Lavender Shortbread   <small>MAKES ABOUT 20 SHORTBREAD COOKIES</small>

Shortbread cookies originated in Scotland. They are a rich and simple cookie made from butter, sugar and flour. The versatile and deliciously plain dough invites creativity when it comes to adding ingredients. This version brings in lavender and lemon flavors.

    2 cups all-purpose flour
    ¼ teaspoon salt
    1 tablespoon dried lavender buds
    1 cup unsalted butter, at room temperature
    ½ cup powdered sugar
    1 tablespoon lemon zest
    1 teaspoon lemon juice

1. Preheat oven to 350°F.
2. Whisk flour, salt and lavender together in a bowl.
3. In another bowl using an electric mixer, cream butter until it is smooth. Add sugar and beat until mixture is light and fluffy.
4. Beat in the lemon zest and juice.
5. Gradually add flour mixture, beating just until it is combined with the butter mixture.
6. Flatten the dough into a disk, wrap in plastic wrap, and chill for at least one hour.
7. On a lightly floured surface, roll cookie dough until it is about ¼-

inch thick.

8. Line two cookie sheets with parchment paper. Using a heart, star or triangle shaped cookie cutter, cut the dough into individual cookies.

9. Place the cookies on cookie sheets and chill in the refrigerator for 15 minutes. (This helps the cookies to hold their shape as they bake.)

10. Bake shortbread in middle of the oven for 8 to 10 minutes, or until golden brown.

Chocolate Lavender Kisses
MAKES 75 KISSES

Meringue is the secret to these sweet, fudgy, lavender-scented cookies. Easy, quick and delicious, they make a perfect homemade gift for the holiday season. For a festive touch, place kisses in a small cellophane bag and tie with a bow—a sweet expression of your love for friends and family.

> **4 egg whites, at room temperature**
> **¼ teaspoon cream of tartar**
> **1 teaspoon pure vanilla extract**
> **Pinch of salt**
> **½ cup unsweetened cocoa powder**
> **¾ cup Lavender Sugar, in all (recipe on page 11)**

1. Preheat oven to 200°F. with the rack in the center of the oven.
2. Line baking sheets with parchment paper or aluminum foil.
3. In a large mixing bowl, beat egg whites, cream of tartar, vanilla, and salt together until foamy.
4. Sift together the cocoa and 2 tablespoons of the lavender sugar and set aside.
5. Add remaining lavender sugar to the egg white mixture, a tablespoon at a time. Beat well after each addition, making sure the sugar is dissolved. Continue to beat until mixture is glossy and makes stiff peaks.
6. Sift the cocoa/sugar mixture over the meringue. Using a spatula, gently fold in the cocoa mixture, just until it is blended.

7. Spoon the meringue mixture into a pastry bag fitted with a ½-inch star tip.
8. Place 1-inch meringue "kisses" onto the lined cookie sheets. (Alternatively, drop the meringue from a tablespoon onto your baking sheet.)
9. Bake the meringues for 1½ hours. The meringues are done when they are crisp and firm to the touch.
10. Turn off the oven and leave the meringues in the oven for another hour to finish drying.
11. Store, covered tightly, in a dry place.

Chocolate and Hazelnut Biscotti   Makes 30 cookies

This Italian cookie gets its hard, dry texture from being baked twice. Perfect for dipping into dessert wine or coffee, these crunchy cookies blend chocolate, hazelnuts and lavender sugar to create a rich, complex flavor.

2 cups all-purpose flour
½ cup cocoa powder
1 teaspoon baking soda
½ teaspoon baking powder
¼ teaspoon salt
6 tablespoon butter, at room temperature
1 cup Lavender Sugar (recipe on page 11)
2 eggs
1 egg white
1 cup hazelnuts, chopped
6 ounces bittersweet chocolate, coarsely chopped

1. Preheat oven to 375°F. Line two baking trays with parchment paper and set aside.
2. Sift flour, cocoa powder, baking soda, baking powder, and salt into a large bowl and set aside.
3. In the bowl of an electric mixer fitted with the paddle attachment, beat butter for 2 minutes. Add sugar and beat on medium speed

until light and fluffy.

4. Add 2 eggs, one at a time, and beat until incorporated.
5. Add the flour mixture gradually and mix until combined.
6. Add the chopped hazelnuts and chocolate and mix with a wooden spoon.
7. Flour your hands (the dough is quite sticky) and turn dough out onto a lightly floured surface. Cut in half and shape each half into a 12-inch log.
8. Place the logs onto the baking trays and flatten them slightly.
9. Lightly beat the egg white and brush the white over the logs. Sprinkle them generously with sugar.
10. Bake the logs for 25 minutes, rotating trays half way through.
11. Transfer the baked logs onto a cutting board and let cool for 20 to 30 minutes.
12. Reduce the oven temperature to 300° F.
13. Cut the logs crosswise to ½-inch thick slices. Place slices on a wire rack and bake again for 30 minutes.
14. Cool. Store in airtight container.

Hot Fudge Sauce with Hint of Lavender   MAKES 2 CUPS

Lavender enhances the flavor of chocolate. This thick and glossy sauce is perfect drizzled over vanilla ice cream, or used as a dipping sauce for strawberries, banana slices, or fresh pineapple chunks.

⅓ cup heavy cream

1 teaspoon lavender buds

½ cup light corn syrup

⅓ cup dark brown sugar, packed

¼ cup unsweetened Dutch-process cocoa powder

¼ teaspoon salt

6 ounces fine-quality bittersweet chocolate, finely chopped

2 tablespoons unsalted butter

1 teaspoon pure vanilla extract

1. In a small saucepan, bring cream to a boil, then remove from heat.
2. Stir in lavender buds, then cover and set aside for 30 minutes. After the mixture has cooled, strain out the lavender buds.
3. Mix cream, sugar, corn syrup, cocoa, salt and half of the chopped chocolate in a 1½-quart saucepan. Stir over moderate heat until the chocolate is melted.
4. Reduce heat and cook at a low boil, stirring occasionally, for 5 minutes, then remove from heat and add butter, vanilla and remaining chocolate. Stir until smooth. Let cool before serving.
5. Store in an airtight container in the refrigerator for up to 1 week.

THE LAVENDER PANTRY

FOLLOWING IS A LIST OF SHOPS THAT FEATURE supplies to stock your lavender pantry. Specialty items include lavender cheeses, syrups, ice cream and even soda pop!

Many of these stores offer their products online, but you may be able to find similar items at your local lavender farm as well. To find a farm near you, visit my website at www.discoverlavender.com. The website also provides an up-to-date list of upcoming lavender festivals, a reading list of lavender-related books, and much more.

The Lavender Pantry

Cheese
Cypress Grove Chèvre
Purple Haze
www.cypressgrovechevre.com
707.825.1100

Rogue Creamery
Cheddar Lavender Cheese
www.roguecreamery.com
866.396.4704

Chocolate Candy
Dagoba Organic Dark Chocolate,
Lavender and Blueberries
www.chocolat-du-monde.com
713.520.5600

Ali'i Kula Lavender
Dark Chocolate Bar
www.aliikulalavender.com
808.878.3004

Gipsons Golden Lavender
Honey Truffles
www.gipsonsgolden.com
707.576.1235

Chutney
Dish D'Lish
Blueberry Lavender Chutney
www.kathycasey.com
206.784.7840

Lou Lou's Garden Plum
Lavender Chutney
www.loulousgarden.com
415.613.8520

Pelindaba Lavender
Lavender Peach Chutney (hot)
www.pelindabalavender.com
866.819.1911

Cookies
Pelindaba Lavender
Lavender Shortbread – mini
www.pelindabalavender.com
866.819.1911

Botanical Bakery
Lavender Tea Cookies
www.botanicalbakery.foodzie.com
customerservice@
botanicalbakery.com

Culinary Lavender Buds
Blue Moon Lavender Farm
Culinary Lavender Buds
www.bluemoonlavender.com
360.681.2271

Purple Haze Organic
Culinary Lavender Buds
phlavender.stores.yahoo.
net/index.html
888.852.6560

Honey
Olympic Lavender Farm
Lavender Honey
www.olympiclavender.com
360.683.4475

Central Coast Lavender
Pure Organic Lavender Honey
www.shop.centralcoastlavender.com
888.327.6528

Jelly & Jam
Hood River Lavender Farms
Vanilla Lavender Pear Jelly
www.lavenderfarms.net

Miller Creek Lavender Farm
Lavender Peach Jam
www.millercrecklavender.com
512.934.1616

Ice Cream
Molly Moon's Homemade Ice
Cream
Lavender Honey Ice Cream
Seattle, Washington
www.mollymoonicecream.com

Snoqualmie Gourmet
Honey Lavender Ice Cream
Maltby, Washington
www.snoqualmiegourmet.com

Nougat
L.A. Burdick
Handmade Nougat Candy
www.burdickchocolate.com
800.229.2419

Montelimar Nougat Bar
www.naturalcandystore.com
800.875.2409

The Lavender Pantry

Seasonings
Clairmont Farms
Culinary Lavender Sea Salt
www.shop.clairmontfarms.com
805.688.7505

Cedarbrook Lavender & Herb
Farm
Lavender Pepper
www.cedarbrooklavender.com
800.470.8423

The Spice House
Lavender Vanilla Sugar
www.thespicehouse.com
847.328.3711

Willow Pond Farm Herbs
and Seasonings
www.willowpondherbs.com
717.642.6387

Soda
DRY Lavender Soda
www.drysoda.com
888.DRY.SODA (379.7632)

Syrup
Sonoma Syrup Co.
Lavender Infused Simple Syrup
www.sonomasyrup.com
707.996.4070

Ali'i Kula Lavender
Lavender Strawberry Syrup
www.aliikulalavender.com
808.878.3004

Tea
Lost Mountain Lavender
Herbal Teas
www.lostmountainlavender.com
888.507.7481

Shooting Star Farm
Lavender Rogue/Loose Tea
www.shootingstarlavender.com
503.728.4236

INDEX

Index

ABOUT THE AUTHOR

Kathy Gehrt enjoys cooking and developing recipes using fresh, local, organic food. She is a member of the International Association of Culinary Professionals and the Pacific Northwest Writers Association.

A sought-after presenter, Kathy has presented her popular cooking demonstration—A Lavender Feast—at the Sequim Lavender Festival and various culinary shops. She speaks at the Vashon Island Farm Tour. Her articles have appeared in *Mother Earth News*, Seattle Farmers Market Alliance's *Market News*, *The Gilded Fork* and Marlene's *Sound Outlook*.

Kathy resides in Seattle, Washington with her husband. Visit her website at www.discoverlavender.com for a list of lavender farms and festivals and to discover new ideas for using this enticing herb.

ABOUT THE PHOTOGRAPHS

IN ADDITION TO CREATING GREAT PICTURES, Shelley Thomas and Brian Smale brought fun and joy to this project.

Shelley, a freelance food stylist and founder of *Early Masters* art school, acted as both artistic director and food stylist; setting up the shots, suggesting props and styling the food. Brian, an award-winning photographer, is well known for his portraits of faces, famous and infamous. His work appears in national magazines such as *Business Week*, *Forbes*, *Fortune*, *London Sunday Times*, and *Rolling Stone*, and on the covers of books by Tom Douglas and Emeril Lagasse.

Shelley and Brian live and work in Seattle.

Ordering Books

To purchase additional copies of *Discover Cooking with Lavender*, visit the "Bookshelf" at www.discoverlavender.com. A significant discount is available when purchasing five or more copies. Single copies are also available.

Questions about ordering?
Email Kathy@discoverlavender.com